Better Homes and Gardens

Snack ATTACK!

Meredith Books
Des Moines, Iowa

Better Homes and Gardens® *Snack Attack!*

Editor: Jennifer Dorland Darling
Contributing Editors: Kristin Bienert, Sheena Chihak, Stephanie Scott
Contributing Graphic Designer: Matthew Eberhart, Evileye Design
Copy Chief: Terri Fredrickson
Publishing Operations Manager: Karen Schirm
Senior Editor, Asset & Information Management: Phillip Morgan
Edit and Design Production Coordinator: Mary Lee Gavin
Editorial Assistant: Cheryl Eckert
Book Production Managers: Pam Kvitne, Marjorie J. Schenkelberg,
   Rick von Holdt, Mark Weaver
Contributing Photographer: Bill Hopkins, Jr.
Contributing Illustrator: Dave Titus
Contributing Copy Editor: Nancy Evans
Contributing Proofreaders: Alison Crouch, Gretchen Kauffman
Test Kitchen Director: Lynn Blanchard
Test Kitchen Home Economists: Elizabeth Burt, R.D.,L.D.; Juliana Hale; Laura Harms, R.D.;
   Maryellyn Krantz; Greg Luna; Jill Moberly; Dianna Nolin; Colleen Weeden; Lori Wilson;
   Charles Worthington

Meredith® Books
Executive Director, Editorial: Gregory H. Kayko
Executive Director, Design: Matt Strelecki
Managing Editor: Amy Tincher-Durik
Senior Associate Design Director: Ken Carlson
Marketing Product Manager: Toye Guinn Cody

Publisher and Editor in Chief: James D. Blume
Editorial Director: Linda Raglan Cunningham
Executive Director, Marketing: Steve Malone
Executive Director, New Business Development: Todd M. Davis
Executive Director, Sales: Ken Zagor
Director, Operations: George A. Susral
Director, Production: Douglas M. Johnston
Director, Marketing: Amy Nichols
Business Director: Jim Leonard

Vice President and General Manager: Douglas J. Guendel

Better Homes and Gardens® Magazine
Deputy Editor, Food and Entertaining: Nancy Hopkins

Meredith Publishing Group
President: Jack Griffin
Executive Vice President: Bob Mate

Meredith Corporation
Chairman and Chief Executive Officer: William T. Kerr
President and Chief Operating Officer: Stephen M. Lacy

In Memoriam: E.T. Meredith III (1933-2003)

All of us at Meredith® Books are dedicated to providing you with the information and ideas you need to create delicious foods. We welcome your comments and suggestions. Write to us at: Meredith Books, Cookbook Editorial Department, 1716 Locust St., Des Moines, IA 50309–3023.

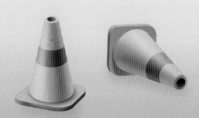

Contents

Your Recipe for Success

BEFORE YOU BEGIN:

➡ Read the recipe from start to finish. Make sure you understand exactly what you're supposed to do. If you don't and can't find the answer in this book, ask an adult to explain.

➡ Check to see that you have enough of all the required ingredients. If you don't, make a list of what you need and ask an adult to help you purchase them.

➡ Gather all the equipment you'll need.

WHILE YOU ARE COOKING:

➡ Measure ingredients accurately.

➡ In general, it's best to finish each step in the recipe before starting the next.

➡ Use good food-safety habits.

WHEN YOU ARE DONE:

➡ Put away all ingredients and equipment. Load dirty dishes in the dishwasher or wash and dry them.
Wipe counters with hot, soapy water. Wipe the table clean.

Introduction

If your stomach is growling even though you scarfed down everything on your plate at lunch, then get a load of *Snack Attack!* a cookbook made just for kids. These awesome snacks will fight off hunger and refuel your body with energy to keep you going.

There aren't any boring grown-up snacks here. *Snack Attack!* is jam-packed with only totally cool recipes for you to munch on. Guzzle down a Groovy Smoothie when you get home from school. Throw a crazy party with Caramel Nutty Corn. Make some Blaze-a-Trail Mix to turn a boring car trip into an awesome adventure. And if you really need to attack your hunger, try the Outrageously Sloppy Joes to make your snack into a meal.

So if you're tired of listening to your stomach growl, it's time to start cooking. Just grab your ingredients and follow the directions. You'll be amazed by what great-tasting stuff you can make.

after-School Favorites

Nacho Melters

NUTRITION FACTS
Per serving: 279 cal., 10 g total fat (6 g sat. fat),
28 mg chol., 298 mg sodium, 19 g carbo.,
2 g fiber, 9 g pro.

Utensils

Sharp knife, if using tomato

Cutting board, if using tomato

Measuring cups

Microwave-safe plate

Measuring spoons

Hot pads

Ingredients

1 small tomato, if you like

4 cups baked tortilla chips (about 3 ounces)

½ of an 8-ounce package shredded Mexican cheese blend (1 cup)

2 to 4 tablespoons salsa

Bacon pieces, cooked, if you like

Dairy sour cream or dairy sour cream dip (any flavor), if you like

How To Make It

1 If using a tomato, use the sharp knife to remove the stem. On the cutting board use the sharp knife to cut the tomato into small pieces. Save until Step 5.

2 On the microwave-safe plate arrange the tortilla chips in a pile to look like a mountain.

3 Sprinkle the cheese over the mountain of chips. Drizzle salsa over the chips.

4 Put the plate in the microwave oven. Microwave on high for 1 to 1½ minutes or until cheese is just melted, giving plate a half-turn halfway through cooking.

5 Use the hot pads to remove the plate from the microwave. If you like, sprinkle with the chopped tomato and/or cooked bacon pieces and top with sour cream or sour cream dip. Makes 4 servings.

What's better than eating a mountain of crunchy, cheesy nachos? Eating it with friends!

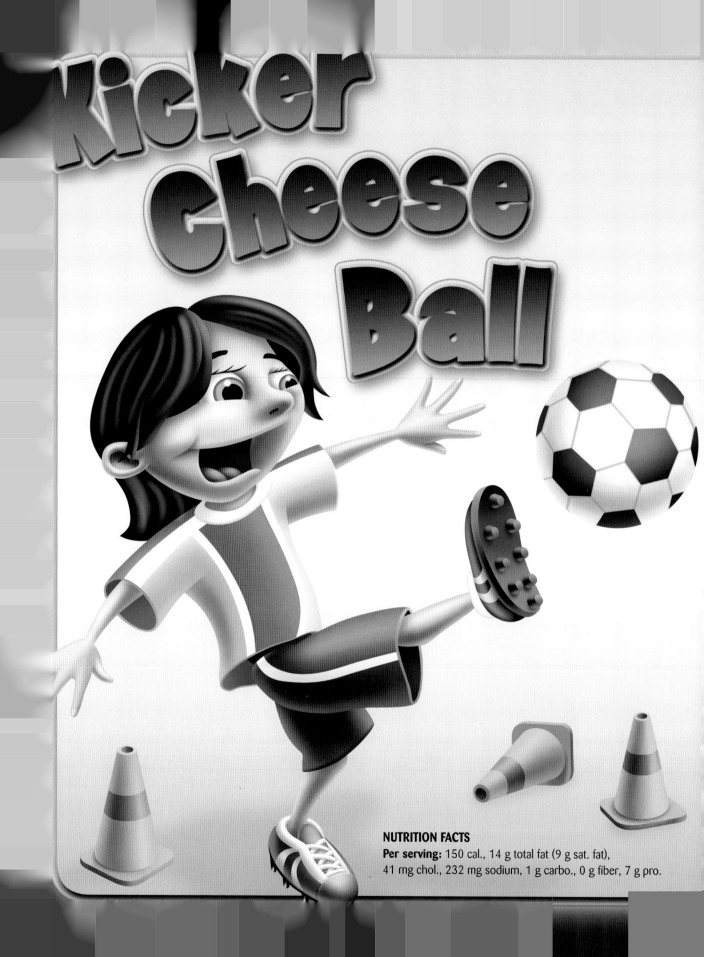

Kicker Cheese Ball

NUTRITION FACTS
Per serving: 150 cal., 14 g total fat (9 g sat. fat),
41 mg chol., 232 mg sodium, 1 g carbo., 0 g fiber, 7 g pro.

Utensils

Measuring cups
Medium mixing bowl
Electric mixer
Rubber scraper
Plastic wrap
Serving plate

Ingredients

1   3-ounce package cream cheese
1¼ cups shredded taco cheese
     Dash bottled hot pepper sauce
     Assorted crackers
     Apple or pear wedges

How To Make It

1   Put cream cheese and 1 cup of the taco cheese in a medium mixing bowl. Let stand at room temperature for 30 minutes.

2   Add bottled hot pepper sauce to the cheese mixture in the mixing bowl. Beat with the electric mixer on medium speed until combined, stopping the mixer occasionally and scraping the sides of the bowl with the rubber scraper. Stop the mixer.

3   Cover the bowl with plastic wrap. Place the bowl in the refrigerator and chill for 4 to 24 hours.

4   Use your hands to shape the cheese mixture into a 3-inch-diameter ball. Roll the ball in the remaining ¼ cup cheese to coat. Place the ball on the serving plate. Let stand about 15 minutes before serving.

5   Serve cheese ball with crackers and apple or pear wedges. Makes ⅔ cup (five 2-tablespoon servings).

Score a perfect goal with this cheesy creation served on top of crackers or fruit slices.

Zippity Pop Popcorn

NUTRITION FACTS
Per serving: 51 cal., 3 g total fat (2 g sat. fat), 7 mg chol., 46 mg sodium, 5 g carbo., 1 g fiber, 1 g pro.

Utensils

Measuring cups

Measuring spoons

Large bowl

Small saucepan or small microwave-safe bowl

Waxed paper, if using microwave

Wooden spoon

2-quart container with tight-fitting lid

Ingredients

8 cups popped popcorn (about ¼ cup unpopped)

2 tablespoons butter or margarine

1 teaspoon chili powder

⅛ teaspoon garlic powder

2 tablespoons grated Parmesan cheese

How To Make It

1 Put popcorn in a large bowl. Remove and throw away all unpopped kernels from popped popcorn. Save popcorn until Step 3.

2 Put the butter in the saucepan. Put the saucepan on a burner. Turn burner to low heat. Heat until butter melts. Turn off burner. Remove saucepan from burner. (Or put butter in the microwave-safe bowl; cover bowl with waxed paper. Microwave on 100% power (high) 20 to 30 seconds or until butter is melted.)

3 Stir chili powder and garlic powder into melted butter with wooden spoon. Drizzle butter mixture over popcorn. Use the wooden spoon to toss the popcorn and coat it as evenly as possible with the butter mixture. Sprinkle with Parmesan cheese; toss again with the wooden spoon.

4 Put the popcorn in the container and cover. Store at room temperature up to 3 days. Makes 10 servings (about 8 cups).

Give your usual popcorn snack some zip with this tasty recipe that's ready in a flash!

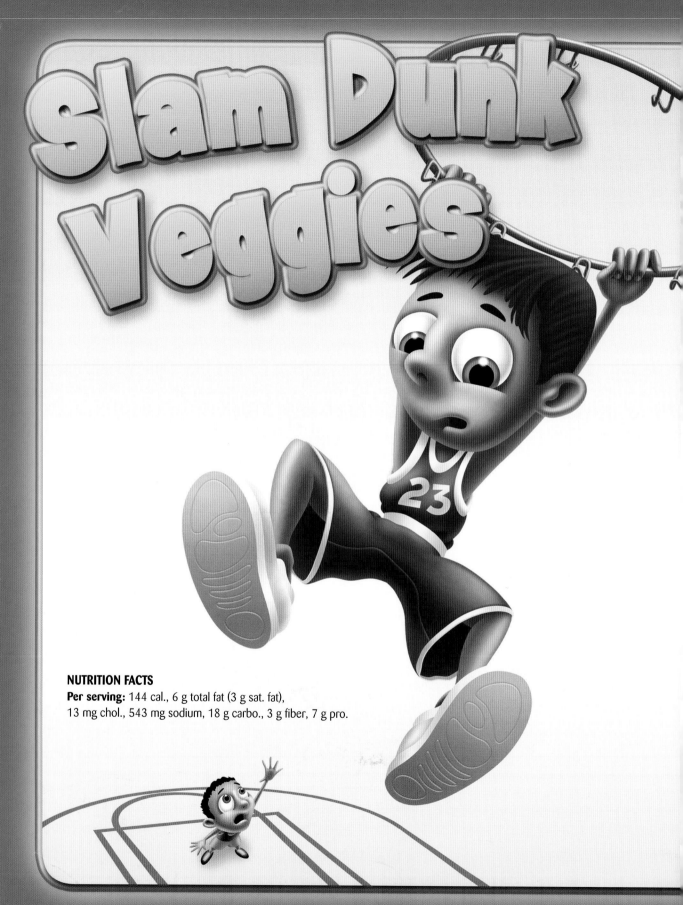

Slam Dunk Veggies

NUTRITION FACTS
Per serving: 144 cal., 6 g total fat (3 g sat. fat),
13 mg chol., 543 mg sodium, 18 g carbo., 3 g fiber, 7 g pro.

Utensils

15×10×1-inch baking pan

Measuring cups

Measuring spoons

Wooden spoon

2 large resealable plastic bags

Hot pads

Small saucepan

Ingredients

Nonstick cooking spray

2/3 cup seasoned fine dry bread crumbs

2 tablespoons grated Parmesan cheese

1/8 teaspoon salt

2 egg whites, slightly beaten

1 tablespoon milk

4 cups cauliflower florets and/or broccoli florets

2 tablespoons butter or margarine, melted

1 15-ounce can pizza sauce

How To Make It

1 Turn on oven to 400°F. Lightly coat the baking pan with cooking spray. Save until Step 2. In a large resealable plastic bag combine bread crumbs, cheese, and salt. In another large plastic bag combine egg whites and milk.

2 Add vegetables to the plastic bag with the egg mixture. Close bag and shake to coat well. Add vegetables to plastic bag with crumb mixture. Close bag and shake to coat well. Place coated vegetables on the prepared baking pan. Drizzle melted butter over vegetables.

3 Bake about 20 minutes or until golden brown, stirring twice with the wooden spoon; use hot pads when removing the pan from the oven each time. Meanwhile, heat the pizza sauce in a saucepan over medium heat.

4 Turn off oven. Remove pan from oven with hot pads. Serve vegetables with warm pizza sauce. Makes 6 servings.

No boring veggies allowed! These veggies have a yummy, crispy coating and get dunked in pizza sauce for ultimate flavor.

Onion Hoops

NUTRITION FACTS
Per serving: 128 cal., 7 g total fat (4 g sat. fat),
16 mg chol., 283 mg sodium, 13 g carbo.,
1 g fiber, 4 g pro.

Utensils

Large baking sheet

Small bowl

Measuring cups

Measuring spoons

Wooden spoon

Waxed paper

Fork

Hot pads

Ingredients

Nonstick cooking spray

$\frac{3}{4}$ cup fine dry bread crumbs

3 tablespoons butter
or margarine, melted

$\frac{1}{4}$ teaspoon salt

2 medium sweet yellow or white
onions, cut into $\frac{1}{4}$-inch
slices and separated into rings

2 egg whites, slightly beaten

How To Make It

1 Turn on oven to 450°F. Lightly coat the baking sheet
with cooking spray. In the small bowl stir together bread
crumbs, melted butter, and salt with the wooden spoon.
Spread about one-fourth of the crumb mixture on a
sheet of waxed paper.

2 Using the fork, dip the onion rings in the egg whites,
coating completely.

3 Roll each onion ring in the bread crumb mixture. Replace
waxed paper and add more of the crumb mixture as
needed.* Place the coated onion rings in a single layer
on the prepared baking sheet.

4 Put baking sheet in the oven for 12 to 15 minutes or
until the onions are tender and the coating is crisp and
golden. Turn off oven. Remove pan from oven with hot
pads. Makes 6 servings.

*Note: The crumb mixture will not stick if combined with the
egg white mixture. Use one-fourth of the crumb mixture
at a time.

You don't have to jump
through hoops to make this
snack. Just mix, dip, bake,
and it's time to dig in!

Fun with Fruit

Here's a new twist on the old PB & J that helps keep the doctor away—you can call it the PB & A!

Berry Bagels

How To Make It

1. Toast a presplit bagel; let it cool a little. Spread bagel halves with cream cheese with strawberries. Top each half with a layer of sliced fresh strawberries.

Fruit and Cheese Spread

How To Make It

1. Put $\frac{1}{2}$ of an 8-ounce tub cream cheese, $\frac{1}{4}$ cup mixed dried fruit bits, and 2 tablespoons shelled sunflower seeds in a small mixing bowl. Stir with a wooden spoon until mixed. Split and toast English muffins. Spread cheese mixture on muffin halves.

apples and Peanut Butter

How To Make It

1. Toast 2 slices of raisin bread. Spread 1 slice of bread with peanut butter. Top with a layer of thinly sliced apple and second slice of raisin bread.

Easy as A-B-C Cookies

Apple
Bana
Chocolat

Fight off your
after-school munchies with
an alphabet you can eat!
Spell out cool words before
you gobble them up!

Utensils

Measuring spoons

Small bowl

Wooden spoon

Table knife

Ingredients

2 ounces reduced-fat cream cheese (tub-style)

1 tablespoon strawberry preserves

Red food coloring, if you like

32 alphabet low-fat plain and/or chocolate shortbread cookies

How To Make It

1 In the bowl stir together the cream cheese and preserves. If you like, stir in a drop of red food coloring. Spread cream cheese mixture on the flat sides of half of the cookies using the table knife. Top with the remaining cookies, flat sides down. Makes 16 cookie sandwiches.

NUTRITION FACTS
Per cookie sandwich: 36 cal., 1 g total fat (1 g sat. fat), 2 mg chol., 38 mg sodium, 6 g carbo., 0 g fiber, 1 g pro.

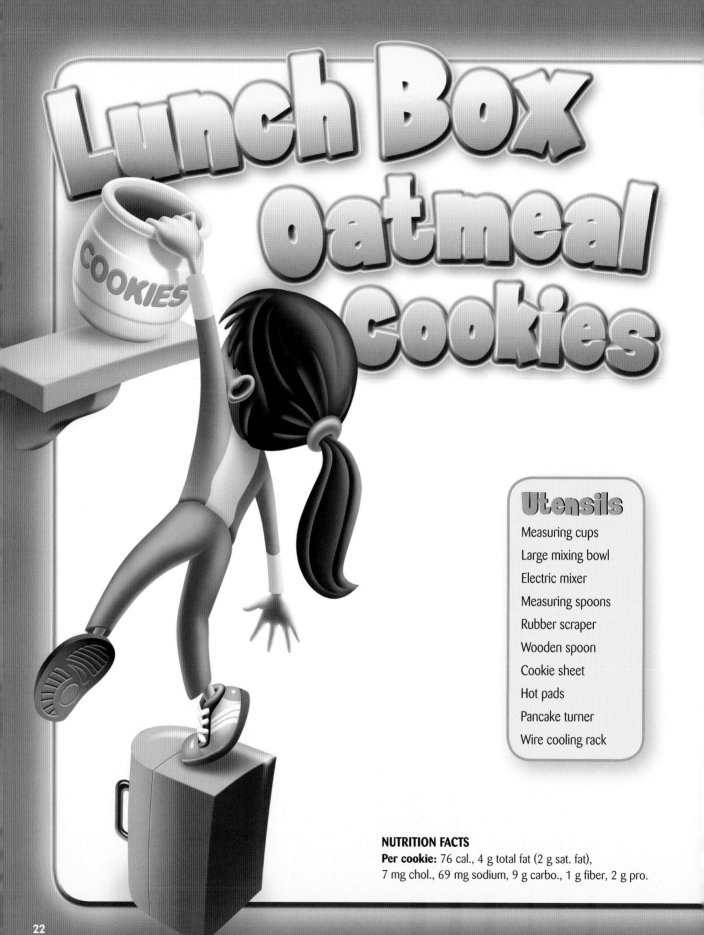

Lunch Box Oatmeal Cookies

Utensils

Measuring cups
Large mixing bowl
Electric mixer
Measuring spoons
Rubber scraper
Wooden spoon
Cookie sheet
Hot pads
Pancake turner
Wire cooling rack

NUTRITION FACTS
Per cookie: 76 cal., 4 g total fat (2 g sat. fat),
7 mg chol., 69 mg sodium, 9 g carbo., 1 g fiber, 2 g pro.

Ingredients

- ½ cup butter or margarine, softened
- ½ cup reduced-fat peanut butter
- ⅓ cup granulated sugar
- ⅓ cup packed brown sugar
- ½ teaspoon baking soda
- 2 egg whites
- ½ teaspoon vanilla
- 1 cup all-purpose flour
- 1 cup quick-cooking rolled oats

How To Make It

1. Turn on oven to 375°F. Put butter and peanut butter in the bowl. Beat with the electric mixer on medium to high speed about 30 seconds or until butter is softened. Stop the mixer. Add granulated sugar, brown sugar, and baking soda. Beat on medium speed until combined, stopping the mixer occasionally and scraping the sides of the bowl with the rubber scraper. Stop the mixer.

2. Add the egg whites and vanilla. Beat on medium speed until combined. Beat in as much flour as you can with the mixer. Stir in any remaining flour with the wooden spoon. Stir in oats.

3. Drop dough by rounded teaspoons 2 inches apart on ungreased cookie sheet. Put the cookie sheet in oven and bake for 7 to 8 minutes or until edges are golden. Cool on cookie sheet for 1 minute. Transfer to a wire rack and let cool. Makes about 40 cookies.

If you fill your lunch box with enough of these chewy cookies to share, you'll be the hit of the school cafeteria!

Groovy Smoothies

NUTRITION FACTS
Per serving: 259 cal., 5 g total fat (3 g sat. fat), 13 mg chol., 113 mg sodium, 49 g carbo., 3 g fiber, 9 g pro.

Utensils

Table knife

Measuring cups

Electric blender

2 serving glasses

Rubber scraper

Ingredients

2   ripe small bananas

1   cup unsweetened whole strawberries, frozen

1   cup vanilla low-fat yogurt

¾   cup milk

How To Make It

1   Remove the peel from the bananas. Using the table knife, cut bananas into chunks.

2   Put banana chunks, frozen strawberries, yogurt, and milk into the blender.

3   Cover blender with the lid and blend on high speed about 1 minute or until mixture is smooth. Turn off blender. Pour drink into glasses. Use rubber scraper to get all of the drink out of the blender. Makes 2 servings.

Skate through hunger by slurping down one of these far-out, fruity smoothies that are good for you too!

Apple Pie Oatmeal

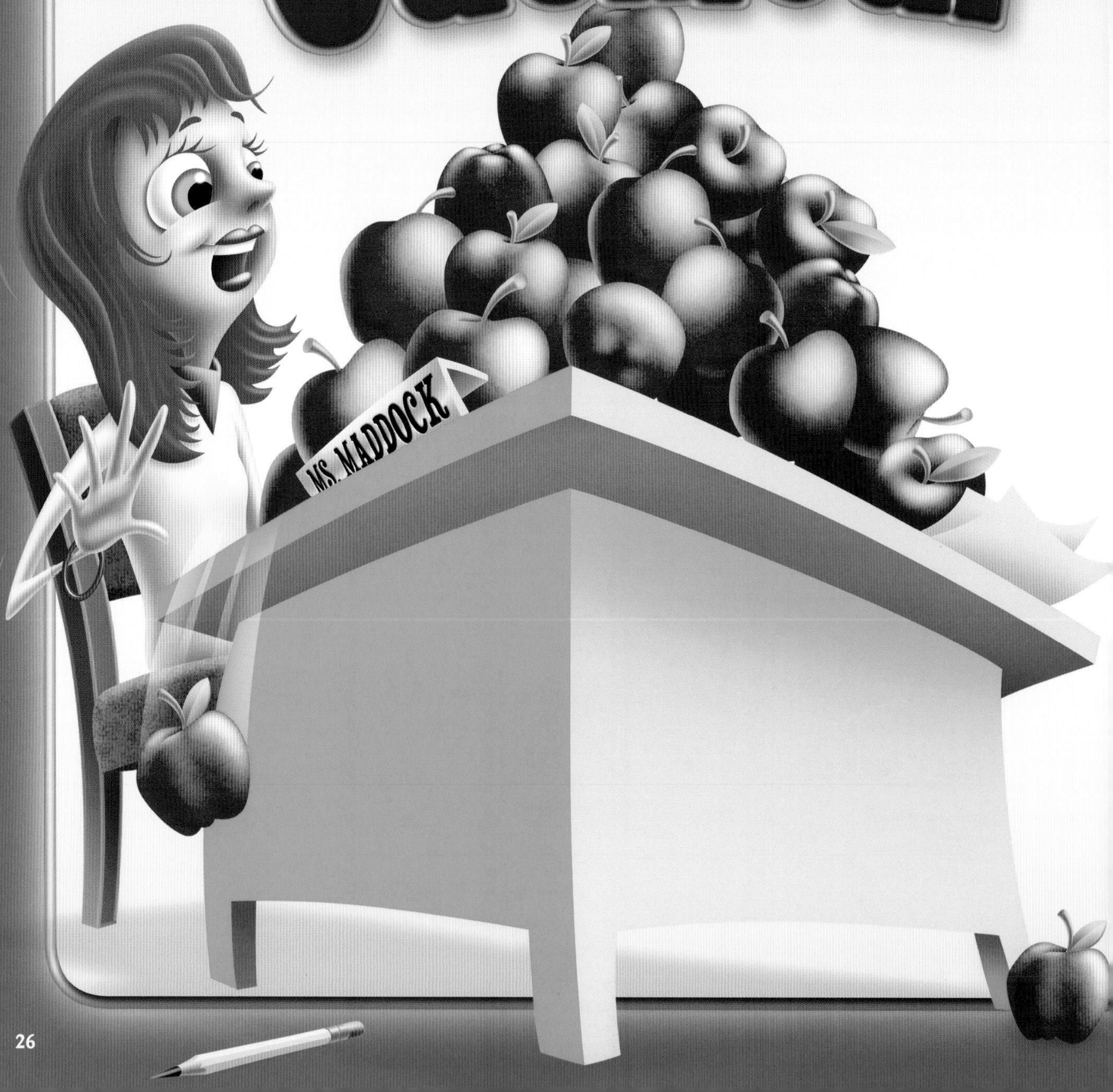

Utensils

Microwave-safe bowl

Measuring cups

Hot pads

Wooden spoon

Measuring spoons

Small saucepan, if using stovetop

Wire cooling rack, if using stovetop

Ingredients

1   0.98-ounce envelope plain instant oatmeal

²⁄₃ cup water

¼   cup unsweetened applesauce

¼   teaspoon apple pie spice

How To Make It

1   Open oatmeal envelope. Pour oatmeal into a microwave-safe bowl. Add the water to the oatmeal. Place bowl in microwave oven. Microwave on 100% power (high) for 1 to 2 minutes or until thickened. Use hot pads to remove bowl from the microwave. Stir with a wooden spoon until mixed. Add applesauce and apple pie spice to oatmeal; stir until mixed. Makes 1 serving.

Stovetop directions: Pour ¹⁄₂ cup water into a small saucepan. Place saucepan on a burner; turn on burner to high heat. Heat water to boiling. Turn off burner. Use hot pads to remove saucepan from heat. Place saucepan on wire rack. Open oatmeal envelope. Pour oatmeal into hot water; stir with a wooden spoon until mixed. Add applesauce and apple pie spice to oatmeal; stir until mixed. Transfer oatmeal to a bowl.

NUTRITION FACTS
Per serving: 131 cal., 2 g total fat (0 g sat. fat), 0 mg chol., 84 mg sodium, 25 g carbo., 4 g fiber, 4 g pro.

Bowl over boring oatmeal with awesome apple flavor. This snack will warm you on a cold day, especially after a long walk from the bus stop!

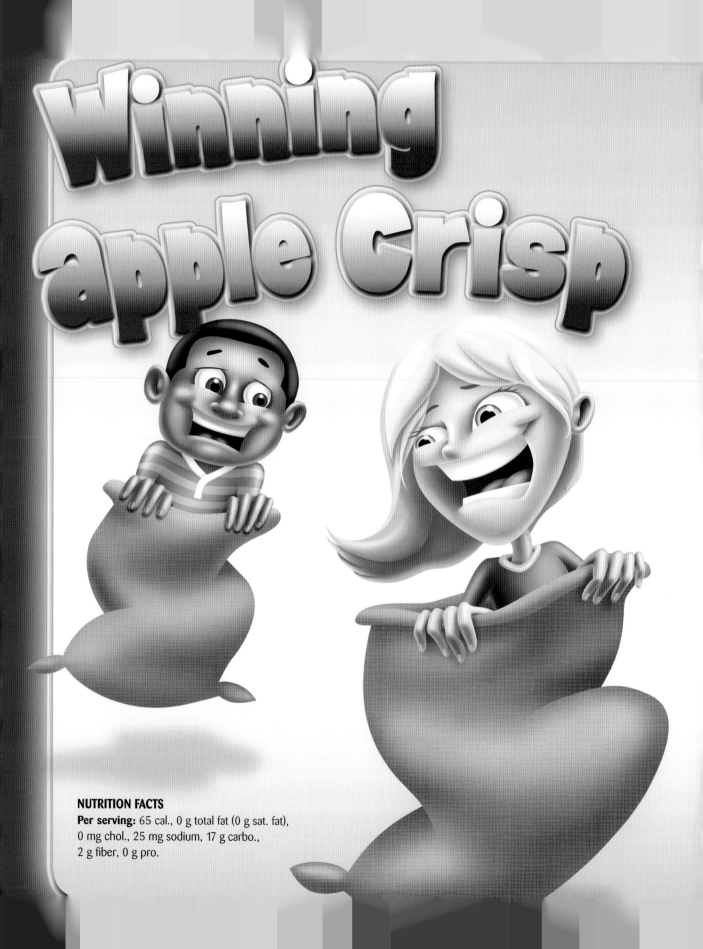

Winning apple Crisp

NUTRITION FACTS
Per serving: 65 cal., 0 g total fat (0 g sat. fat),
0 mg chol., 25 mg sodium, 17 g carbo.,
2 g fiber, 0 g pro.

Utensils

Small spoons

Microwave-safe 6-ounce custard cup or small bowl

Measuring spoons

Hot pads

Ingredients

1 4-ounce snack-size container unsweetened applesauce

1/8 teaspoon apple pie spice or ground cinnamon

2 tablespoons reduced-sugar sugar-coated cornflakes or round toasted multigrain cereal

1 tablespoon sliced almonds, pecan pieces, or walnut pieces, if you like

How To Make It

1 Uncover applesauce container. Spoon applesauce into custard cup or small bowl. Use a small spoon to stir in apple pie spice. Place custard cup with applesauce in the microwave. Microwave, uncovered, on 100% power (high) for 15 to 30 seconds until warm. Use hot pads to carefully remove custard cup from microwave; stir applesauce. Sprinkle cereal over warm applesauce. If you like, sprinkle with nuts. Eat while warm. Makes 1 serving.

Strawberry-Apple Crisp: Make as directed above, except do not add the apple pie spice to the applesauce. Instead, stir 1 teaspoon of low-sugar strawberry preserves into the cold applesauce. Heat and serve as directed in Step 1.

Use this recipe to beat a growling stomach and be champion of the kitchen. Add the almonds if you want to go a little nuts!

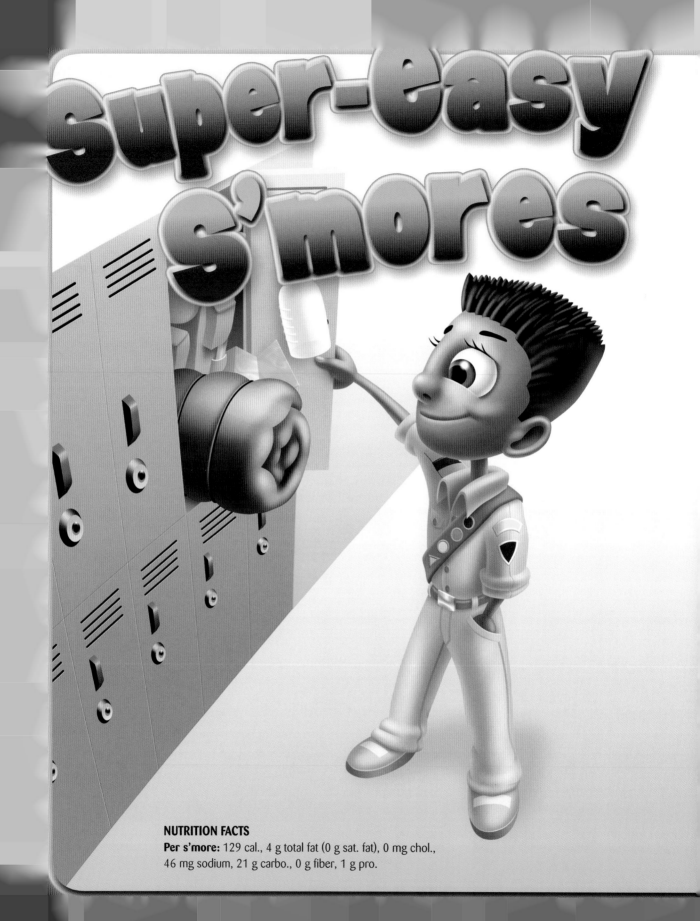

Super-Easy S'mores

NUTRITION FACTS
Per s'more: 129 cal., 4 g total fat (0 g sat. fat), 0 mg chol.,
46 mg sodium, 21 g carbo., 0 g fiber, 1 g pro.

Utensils

Measuring spoons
2 table knives
Microwave-safe plate

Ingredients

8   regular or chocolate graham cracker squares

3   tablespoons chocolate-hazelnut spread

3   tablespoons marshmallow creme

How To Make It

1   Place graham cracker squares on a work surface. Use table knife to spread 4 squares with chocolate-hazelnut spread. Spread remaining graham cracker squares with marshmallow creme. Place graham crackers, marshmallow sides down, on top of chocolate-hazelnut spread. Place on the microwave-safe plate.

2   Microwave, uncovered, on 100% power (high) for 30 seconds. (If you want to heat the s'mores one or two at a time, microwave one s'more on 100% power [high] for 10 seconds or two s'mores for 20 seconds.) Serve at once. Makes 4 s'mores.

Peanut Butter S'mores: Prepare as directed, except use chocolate graham cracker squares and substitute peanut butter for the chocolate-hazelnut spread.

After hiking the hallways at school and backpacking home, it is time for a special treat that'll have you asking for s'more!

Travelin' Food

Stop 'n' Go Cookies

Utensils

Measuring cups
Measuring spoons
Medium bowl
Table knife
Large mixing bowl
Electric mixer
Rubber scraper

Wooden spoon
Cookie sheet
Wooden sticks, if using
Hot pads
Pancake turner
Wire cooling rack

Ingredients

1½ cups all-purpose flour

½ cup unsweetened cocoa powder

¼ teaspoon baking soda

¼ teaspoon baking powder

¼ teaspoon salt

½ cup butter, softened

1 cup granulated sugar

1 egg

1½ teaspoons vanilla

Red, yellow, and green candy-coated milk chocolate pieces or candy-coated peanut butter and chocolate pieces

How To Make It

1 Turn on oven to 350°F. Put the flour, cocoa powder, baking soda, baking powder, and salt in the medium bowl. Save until Step 4.

2 Cut up the butter using the table knife. Put butter in the large bowl. Beat with the electric mixer on medium speed for 30 seconds or until butter is softened. Stop the mixer.

3 Add the sugar. Beat on medium speed until combined, stopping the mixer occasionally and scraping the bowl with the rubber scraper. Stop the mixer. Add egg and vanilla. Beat on medium speed until combined.

4 Add the flour mixture $\frac{1}{2}$ cup at a time, beating as much of it in as you can with the mixer. Stop the mixer. Stir in as much of the flour mixture as you can with the wooden spoon. If necessary, use your hands to work the remaining flour mixture into the dough.

5 For each cookie, shape 1 tablespoon of dough into a $2\frac{1}{2}$x$1\frac{1}{4}$-inch rectangle on the ungreased cookie sheet. Leave about 2 inches between cookies. If you like, push a wooden stick halfway into a short side of each rectangle.

6 Press red, yellow, and green candy-coated piece into each rectangle for the lights on the stoplight.

7 Put the cookie sheet in oven. Bake for 8 to 10 minutes or until the cookie edges are firm. Use the hot pads to remove cookie sheet from oven. Let cookies remain on cookie sheet for 1 minute. Use the pancake turner to transfer cookies to the cooling rack. Repeat with remaining dough. If using just 1 cookie sheet, let it cool between batches. Turn off oven. Makes 26 cookies.

These clever cookies are perfect for driving away hunger on long road trips or days full of running errands with Mom or Dad!

NUTRITION FACTS
Per cookie: 93 cal., 4 g total fat (2 g sat. fat), 18 mg chol., 158 mg sodium, 14 g carbo., 1 g fiber, 1 g pro.

Double-Decker Delights

Utensils

Measuring spoons

Small bowl

Spoon

Cutting board

Sharp knife

3- to 3½-inch round
 cookie cutter

Table knife

Measuring cups,
 if using nuts

NUTRITION FACTS
Per serving: 177 cal.,
6 g total fat (3 g sat. fat),
13 mg chol., 419 mg sodium,
26 g carbo., 2 g fiber, 6 g pro.

Ingredients

½ of an 8-ounce tub light cream cheese, softened

½ teaspoon finely shredded orange peel

2 to 3 teaspoons fat-free milk

3 8-inch whole wheat or plain flour tortillas

1 medium apple, pear, and/or banana

¼ cup chopped almonds, pecans, or walnuts, toasted, if you like

How To Make It

1 Put cream cheese, orange peel, and milk in the small bowl and stir with the spoon. Save until Step 2. If using apple or pear, on the cutting board use the sharp knife to core and thinly slice the apple and/or pear. If using banana, peel and use cutting board and sharp knife to slice.

2 Use the cookie cutter to cut tortillas into 12 rounds (discard scraps). Spread cream cheese mixture onto rounds using the table knife. Save until Step 3.

3 Place half of the fruit slices on 4 of the tortilla rounds. If you like, sprinkle with half the nuts. Add another layer of tortilla, half of the fruit slices, and, if you like, half the nuts. Top with remaining tortilla rounds, cream cheese sides down. Makes 4 servings.

An empty stomach is no monkey business. These double-deckers are stacked to the max so you aren't stuck running on empty.

Dip and Eat Lunch

NUTRITION FACTS
Per serving: 140 cal.,
7 g total fat (3 g sat. fat), 37 mg chol.,
710 mg sodium, 7 g carbo., 1 g fiber, 13 g pro

Utensils

Cutting board

Sharp knife

Measuring cups

Measuring spoons

2-cup plastic container with lid or 1-quart resealable plastic bag

Small container with lid

Small spoon

Ingredients

1 ounce smoked turkey sausage

1 ounce mozzarella or provolone cheese

1 ounce Italian bread

½ of a small zucchini, 1 carrot, ½ cup broccoli florets, ½ of a medium green sweet pepper, and/or ½ cup grape or cherry tomatoes

¼ cup tomato sauce

⅛ teaspoon dried Italian seasoning

Dash garlic powder

How To Make It

1 On the cutting board use the sharp knife to cut sausage into bite-size slices. On the same cutting board use the sharp knife to cut the cheese into bite-size cubes. On the cutting board use the sharp knife to cut the bread into bite-size pieces. On the cutting board use the sharp knife to cut the zucchini, carrot, broccoli, sweet pepper, and/or tomatoes into bite-size pieces.

2 Put sausage, cheese, bread, and vegetables into the 2-cup plastic container or into the plastic bag. Put the lid on the container or seal the bag; chill for 1 to 6 hours.

3 Put the tomato sauce, Italian seasoning, and garlic powder in the small container. Stir with a small spoon until combined. Put the lid on the container. Chill container up to 6 hours. To eat, dip the sausage, cheese, bread, and vegetable pieces in the tomato mixture. Makes 1 serving.

When you're on the go, finger foods like these delicious dunkers make the perfect snack!

Food on a Stick

NUTRITION FACTS
Per kabob: 117 cal.,
10 g total fat (4 g sat. fat), 24 mg chol.,
520 mg sodium, 2 g carbo., 0 g fiber, 5 g pro.

Utensils

Cutting board

Sharp knife

Measuring cups

Melon baller, if using

Twelve 6-inch bamboo skewers

Serving plate

Plastic wrap

Ingredients

6 ounces salami

6 ounces mozzarella or provolone cheese

1½ cups cantaloupe and/or honeydew melon

1 cup purchased large pitted herbed green olives* and/or large pitted ripe olives

¾ cup cherry tomatoes

How To Make It

1 On the cutting board use the sharp knife to slice salami and cube the cheese. Use the mellon baller to ball the cantaloupe or a sharp knife to cut it into chunks.

2 On six of the bamboo skewers alternately thread salami, cheese, and melon balls. On the other six skewers thread salami, cheese, olives, and cherry tomatoes. Place on a serving plate. Cover with plastic wrap and chill up to 2 hours before serving. Makes 12 kabobs.

*NOTE: Herbed green olives can be found in Italian markets. However, if you want to make your own, here's how. In a small bowl combine 1 cup large pitted green olives, pimiento-stuffed olives, and/or pitted ripe olives; 1½ teaspoons olive oil; 1 clove garlic, minced; ½ teaspoon dried Italian seasoning, crushed; and ⅛ teaspoon crushed red pepper. Stir until olives are evenly coated. Cover and chill for at least 2 hours.

Stack pieces of meat, cheese, and melon on a stick for a yummy car-ride kabob!

Wonton Chips

NUTRITION FACTS
Per serving (4 chips): 69 cal., 2 g total fat (1 g sat. fat),
2 mg chol., 116 mg sodium, 9 g carbo., 0 g fiber, 2 g pro.

Utensils

Baking sheet

Foil, if making ruffled chips

Sharp knife

Small bowl

Measuring spoons

Spoon

Pastry brush

Measuring cups

Hot pads

Pancake turner

Wire cooling rack

Ingredients

Nonstick cooking spray

30 wonton wrappers

2 tablespoons olive oil

1 clove garlic, minced

½ teaspoon dried basil, crushed

¼ cup grated Parmesan or Romano cheese

How To Make It

1 Turn on oven to 350°F. Lightly coat a baking sheet with cooking spray. If you like, for ruffled chips, line baking sheet with foil. Shape foil to make ridges. Lightly coat foil with cooking spray. Save baking sheet until Step 2.

2 Use a sharp knife to cut wonton wrappers in half diagonally to make 60 triangles. Arrange one-third of the triangles in a single layer on the prepared baking sheet. If making ruffled chips, place wonton triangles on foil, draping over foil ridges.

3 In a small bowl stir together the olive oil, garlic, and basil. Use the pastry brush to lightly brush the wonton triangles with one-third of the oil mixture; sprinkle with one-third of the cheese.

4 Put baking sheet in oven. Bake for 8 minutes or until golden. Use hot pads to remove baking sheet from oven. Use the pancake turner to transfer chips to cooling rack; cool completely. Repeat with the remaining wonton triangles, oil mixture, and cheese. Turn off oven. Makes 60 chips (15 servings).

Travel to a foreign land on your next snacking adventure. Wonton wrappers, used in Chinese cooking, make awesome chips to take along wherever you travel!

Pretzel Paddles

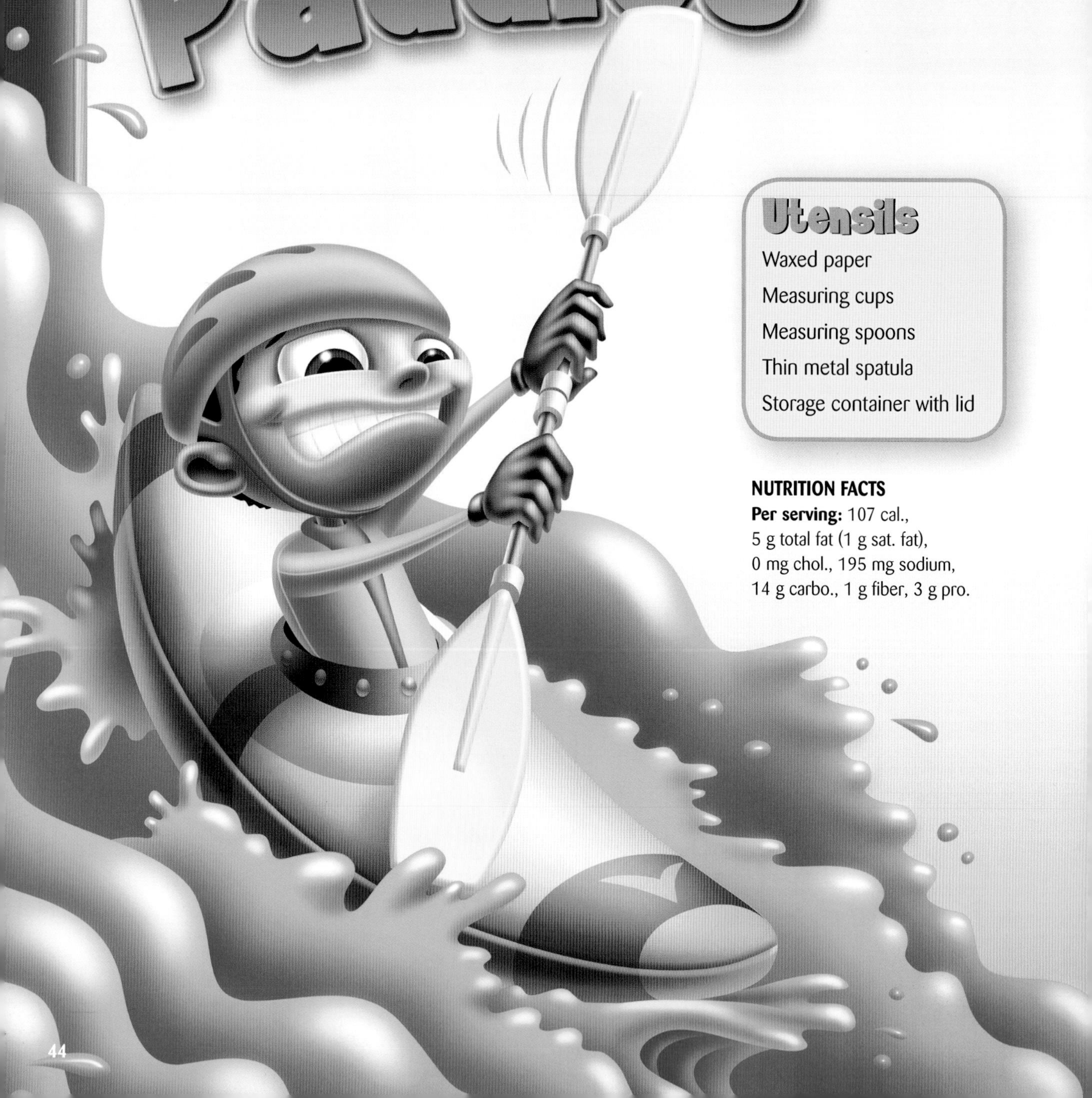

Utensils

Waxed paper
Measuring cups
Measuring spoons
Thin metal spatula
Storage container with lid

NUTRITION FACTS
Per serving: 107 cal.,
5 g total fat (1 g sat. fat),
0 mg chol., 195 mg sodium,
14 g carbo., 1 g fiber, 3 g pro.

44

Ingredients

¾ cup reduced-sugar chocolate-flavored puffed corn cereal and/or sweetened fruit-flavored round toasted cereal

2 tablespoons creamy peanut butter

4 pretzel rods

How To Make It

1 Lay the waxed paper on the counter. Spread desired cereal on waxed paper. Set aside. Using the metal spatula, spread peanut butter in a thin layer over half of each pretzel rod. Roll each rod in the cereal so it sticks to the peanut butter. Eat right away or put logs in an airtight container and store at room temperature for up to 1 day. Makes 4 servings.

Take these sweet and salty pretzel sticks on your next adventure and you'll be able to lick any snack attack!

PB Crunchers

NUTRITION FACTS
Per snack: 163 cal., 9 g total fat (3 g sat. fat),
0 mg chol., 101 mg sodium, 19 g carbo.,
1 g fiber, 5 g pro.

Utensils

Baking sheet

Waxed paper

Measuring cups

Large bowl

Wooden spoon

Hot pads

Medium microwave-safe bowl

Hot pads

Saucepan, if melting peanut
  butter on top of the stove

2 spoons

Storage container with lid

Ingredients

1 3-ounce can chow mein
     noodles (2 cups)

1 cup cornflakes

½ cup raisins

1 12-ounce package
     peanut butter-flavored
     pieces (2 cups)

How To Make It

1 Cover the baking sheet with waxed paper. Save until Step 5.

2 Put the chow mein noodles, cornflakes, and raisins in the large bowl. Stir with the wooden spoon until mixed. Save until Step 4.

3 Put the peanut butter-flavored pieces in the microwave-safe bowl. Microwave, uncovered, on 100% power (high) for 45 seconds. Use hot pads to remove the bowl from the microwave oven. Stir with the wooden spoon until smooth. If necessary, microwave for 15 to 45 seconds more, stirring after every 15 seconds. (Or put the peanut butter pieces in the saucepan. Put the pan on a burner. Turn the burner to low heat. Cook until the pieces are melted, stirring all the time with the wooden spoon. Turn off the burner. Remove the pan from the heat.)

4 Pour the melted peanut butter mixture over the noodle mixture. Quickly stir the mixture with the wooden spoon until all of the mixture is coated.

5 Working quickly, use 2 spoons to drop the mixture onto the prepared baking sheet. Let stand at room temperature until firm. Transfer the crunchers to the container. Cover tightly and store in the refrigerator for up to 5 days. Makes 15 snacks.

If you don't have a lot of time before you hit the road, these crunchy snacks are a great choice because they're ready lickety-split!

Blaze-a-Trail Mix

NUTRITION FACTS
Per ½-cup serving: 199 cal.,
10 g total fat (3 g sat. fat), 0 mg chol.,
81 mg sodium, 26 g carbo.,
2 g fiber, 5 g pro.

Utensils

Measuring cups

Large storage
  container with lid

Ingredients

2 cups honey graham
  cereal

1 cup tiny marshmallows

1 cup peanuts

½ cup semisweet
  chocolate pieces

½ cup raisins

How To Make It

1 In a storage container combine all the
  ingredients. Cover and shake to mix.
  Store in a cool, dry place for up to
  2 weeks. Makes 5 cups.

Need an energy
boost before you start your
explorations? Grab a handful of
this mix and hit the trail!

Radical Ride Mix

Utensils

Measuring cups
Measuring spoons
Medium saucepan
Wooden spoon
13×9×2-inch baking pan
Hot pads
Foil
Large resealable plastic bag
or storage container with lid

NUTRITION FACTS
Per serving: 482 cal., 25 g total fat (8 g sat. fat), 15 mg chol., 69 mg sodium, 57 g carbo., 7 g fiber, 13 g pro.

Ingredients

¼ cup apple jelly or your favorite flavor jelly

3 tablespoons granulated sugar

2 tablespoons butter or margarine

½ teaspoon ground cinnamon

1 cup rolled oats

½ cup peanuts or slivered almonds

¼ cup shelled sunflower seeds

¼ cup coconut

How To Make It

1 Turn on the oven to 325°F.

2 Put jelly, sugar, butter, and cinnamon in the saucepan. Put pan on a burner. Turn burner to low heat. Cook until the butter is melted and sugar is dissolved, stirring all of the time with the wooden spoon. Turn off burner. Remove pan from burner.

3 Add the oats, peanuts or almonds, sunflower seeds, and coconut to the mixture in the saucepan. Stir with the wooden spoon until mixed.

4 Pour the mixture into the ungreased baking pan. Spread the mixture in an even layer with the wooden spoon. Put the baking pan in the oven. Twice during baking, open the oven door and use hot pads to pull out the oven rack slightly; stir the mixture with the wooden spoon. Bake for 20 to 25 minutes or until lightly browned. Turn off the oven. Use hot pads to remove the pan from the oven.

5 Tear off a piece of foil that measures about 14×12 inches. Pour the mixture from the pan onto the foil, using hot pads. Cool completely.

6 To store, place the mixture in the plastic bag or container; seal or cover tightly. Store in a cool, dry place for up to 2 weeks. Makes 4 cups.

For a totally rad ride, take some of this sweet, crunchy mixture along with you and chow down whenever hunger strikes!

Carmel Nutty Corn

NUTRITION FACTS
Per $\frac{1}{2}$-cup serving: 191 cal., 12 g total fat
(2 g sat. fat), 0 mg chol., 19 g carbo.,
2 g fiber, 3 g pro.

Utensils

Measuring cups

Measuring spoons

13x9x2-inch baking pan

Small saucepan or small
  microwave-safe bowl

Waxed paper,
  if using microwave oven

Hot pads

Wooden spoon

Serving bowl

Storage container with lid

Ingredients

6   cups popped popcorn
    (about 3 tablespoons
    unpopped)

3   tablespoons butter
    or margarine

¼   cup light-colored
    corn syrup

1   tablespoon molasses

1   cup dry-roasted cashews,
    peanuts, or shelled
    sunflower seeds

How To Make It

1   Turn on oven to 325°F. Place the popped popcorn in the
    baking pan. Save until Step 4.

2   Put margarine in the saucepan. Put saucepan on a burner.
    Turn burner to low heat. Heat until butter melts. Turn off
    burner. Remove saucepan from burner. Or put butter in
    the microwave-safe bowl. Cover bowl with waxed paper.
    Microwave on 100% power (high) for 20 to 30 seconds or
    until margarine is melted. Using hot pads, remove bowl from
    microwave oven.

3   Stir corn syrup and molasses into melted butter using the
    wooden spoon.

4   Slowly pour the corn syrup mixture over popcorn in baking
    pan. Use the wooden spoon to toss the popcorn and coat it as
    evenly as possible with the corn syrup mixture.

5   Put baking pan in oven. Bake for 15 minutes, stirring with a
    wooden spoon about every 5 minutes; use hot pads when
    removing the pan from the oven each time. Turn off oven.
    Remove pan from oven with hot pads.

6   Pour caramel corn into the serving bowl. Stir in nuts or
    sunflower seeds with the wooden spoon. Let caramel corn
    cool. Store in a tightly covered container at room temperature.
    Makes about 4 cups.

Feeling nutty?
Here's the munchie for you—
sweet, caramelly popcorn with
a whole cup of nuts, and
there's plenty to share!

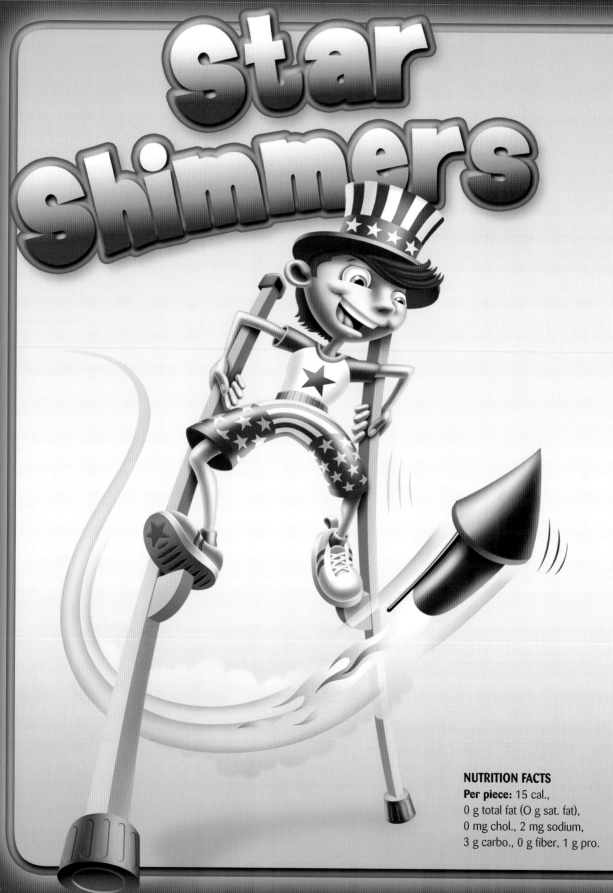

NUTRITION FACTS
Per piece: 15 cal.,
0 g total fat (O g sat. fat),
0 mg chol., 2 mg sodium,
3 g carbo., 0 g fiber, 1 g pro.

Utensils

8x8x2-inch baking pan

Foil

Measuring cups

Medium saucepan

Wooden spoon

Hot pads

Plastic wrap

Cutting board

1½-inch star-shape or other shape cookie cutter or table knife

Ingredients

1½ cups lemon-lime carbonated beverage

3 envelopes unflavored gelatin

1 6-ounce can frozen orange juice or lemonade concentrate, partly thawed

Small decorative candies, if you like

How To Make It

1 Line the baking pan with the foil so foil covers the bottom and sides of the pan. Press the foil into the pan where the sides and the bottom meet. Smooth out the foil with your fingers to remove wrinkles. Save until Step 3.

2 Pour the carbonated beverage into the saucepan. Sprinkle the gelatin over the beverage. Let stand for 1 minute. Put the pan on the burner. Turn the burner to high. Heat until mixture begins to boil, stirring all the time with the wooden spoon. Boil and stir until the gelatin dissolves. Turn off burner. Use hot pads to remove saucepan from burner.

3 Open the can of frozen juice concentrate and combine with the hot gelatin. Stir until the frozen juice concentrate is completely melted. Pour mixture into the foil-lined pan. Cover pan with plastic wrap. Place pan in the refrigerator. Chill about 4 hours or until firm.

4 Turn the pan upside down on the cutting board to remove the gelatin. Use the cookie cutter or the table knife to cut the gelatin into shapes. If you like, sprinkle with candies. Makes 36 pieces.

These tangy, fruity treats will be the star of your party table. Make them shimmer with your favorite candies or leave them plain; they're cool either way!

abracadabra Sticks

Utensils

Measuring cups

Measuring spoons

Small microwave-safe bowl

Hot pads

Wooden spoon, if using
stovetop method

Small saucepan, if using
stovetop method

Spoon

Waxed paper

Resealable plastic bag, if piping
melted coating on wands

Storage container with lid

Ingredients

½ cup vanilla milk pieces
or 3 ounces vanilla-flavored
candy coating, chopped

1 teaspoon shortening

15 long pretzel sticks

Decorative candies or
colored sugars, if you like

Paste food coloring,
if you like*

How To Make It

1 Place the vanilla milk pieces and shortening in a small microwave-safe bowl. Microwave on 100% power for 1 to 2 minutes or until the mixture is softened enough to stir smooth. Remove the bowl from the microwave oven using the hot pads. The mixture won't seem melted until stirred.

2 Hold a pretzel over the melted mixture. Carefully spoon melted mixture over the end of the pretzel stick. Place the stick on a sheet of waxed paper. If you like, sprinkle the melted mixture with decorative candies or sugars. Repeat with remaining sticks and melted mixture. Let stand at room temperature until the melted mixture becomes firm (about 1 hour).

3 If desired, use paste food coloring to tint any remaining coating. Place in a heavy self-sealing plastic bag; cut off a tiny corner of bag. Pipe melted colored candy coating onto dipped sticks. Or dip coated end of dipped stick into a contrasting-color candy coating and sprinkle with colored sugar or decorative candies. Chill about 1 hour. To store place sticks in layers in an airtight container, separating layers with waxed paper. Store at room temperature for up to 1 week. Makes 10 sticks.

Stovetop directions: Put the vanilla milk pieces and shortening in the saucepan. Place the saucepan on a burner. Turn the burner to low heat. Heat the pieces or coating until smooth, stirring all the time with the wooden spoon. Turn the burner off. Use hot pads to remove saucepan

NUTRITION FACTS
Per serving: 100 cal., 4 g total fat (2 g sat. fat), 3 mg chol., 140 mg sodium, 15 g carbo., 0 g fiber, 2 g pro.

Make snack time magical with these decorated pretzels. What spells will you cast?

Party Punch

NUTRITION FACTS
Per serving: 93 cal., 0 g total fat (0 g sat. fat.),
0 mg chol., 7 mg sodium, 24 g carbo.,
0 g fiber, 0 g pro.

Utensils

Measuring cups

Large pitcher with lid

Wooden spoon

Serving glasses

Ingredients

2 cups cherry juice blend

1 6-ounce can frozen lemonade concentrate, thawed

3 11-ounce bottles sparkling water with cherry flavor

Crushed ice

How To Make It

1 Pour the cherry juice blend and lemonade concentrate into the pitcher; stir with the wooden spoon until mixed. Cover and chill until serving time.

2 Just before serving, carefully pour the sparkling water into the cherry juice mixture.

3 Fill glasses with crushed ice. Pour the cherry juice mixture into the glasses. Makes ten 6-ounce servings.

Gulp down a glass of this colorful thirst quencher at your next bash and you're sure to have a blast!

Fruit Sundae Cones

Utensils

Measuring cups

Electric blender

Large bowl

Spoon

Ingredients

¾ cup cut-up strawberries

3 cups cut-up fruits such as apples, bananas, cherries, seedless red grapes, kiwifruits, plums, and/or peaches

6 large waffle cones

¼ cup toasted coconut, if you like

How To Make It

1 Place strawberries in a blender; cover and blend until smooth. Place desired fruit in bowl; gently toss together. Spoon fruit into cones. Drizzle with the blended strawberries. If you like, top with coconut. Makes 6 servings.

Have your parents stock up on a bunch of different fruits so guests at your party can add their favorites for a fruity treat that rocks!

NUTRITION FACTS
Per serving: 105 cal., 1 g total fat (0 g sat. fat), 0 mg chol., 25 mg sodium, 24 g carbo., 2 g fiber, 1 g pro.

Valentine Berry Parfait

NUTRITION FACTS
Per parfait: 266 cal., 13 g total fat (7 g sat. fat),
45 mg chol., 301 mg sodium, 34 g carbo., 1 g fiber, 4 g pro.

Utensils

Cutting board

Serrated knife

Measuring cups

Sharp knife,
  if using strawberries

Small bowl

Rubber scraper

2 serving glasses

Ingredients

2 1-inch-thick angel
     food cake slices

¾ cup fresh strawberries
     and/or raspberries

1 4-ounce container
     vanilla pudding

¼ cup whipped cream
     or thawed frozen
     whipped dessert topping

1 drop red food coloring,
     if you like

How To Make It

1 Place the cake slices on the cutting board. Using the serrated knife, cut the cake into 1-inch cubes. Save until Step 4.

2 If using strawberries, place them on the cutting board. Use the sharp knife to remove the green stems. Slice the strawberries, cutting from top of each berry to the bottom. Save until Step 4.

3 Put the vanilla pudding and whipped cream in the bowl. Use the rubber scraper to gently stir the whipped cream into the pudding. If you like, stir in red food coloring.

4 Place one-fourth of the cake cubes in the bottom of each glass. Add one-fourth of the berries to each glass. Top with one-fourth of the pudding mixture. Repeat the layers. Serve the parfaits immediately. Makes 2 parfaits.

Show off your sweet side with these pretty desserts. Share one with someone special!

Frankie's Fun Mix

NUTRITION FACTS
Per ½-cup serving: 161 cal.,
6 g total fat (1 g sat. fat),
1 mg chol., 182 mg sodium,
25 g carbo., 2 g fiber, 3 g pro.

Utensils

Measuring cups

Large bowl

Wooden spoon

Storage container with lid

Ingredients

2½ cups coarsely
  crushed blue
  corn chips

1 cup corn nuts

1 cup raisins

1 cup pretzel sticks

1 cup canned
  potato sticks

1 cup cheese sticks

½ cup shelled pistachio
  nuts or peanuts

How To Make It

1 In a large bowl toss together corn chips, corn
nuts, raisins, pretzels, potato sticks, cheese sticks,
and nuts.

2 Store in an airtight container in a cool, dry place
up to 2 weeks. Makes about 8 cups.

Play a mad scientist
by mixing the crunchy pieces
of this recipe together to
make a Halloween party
"spooktacular"!

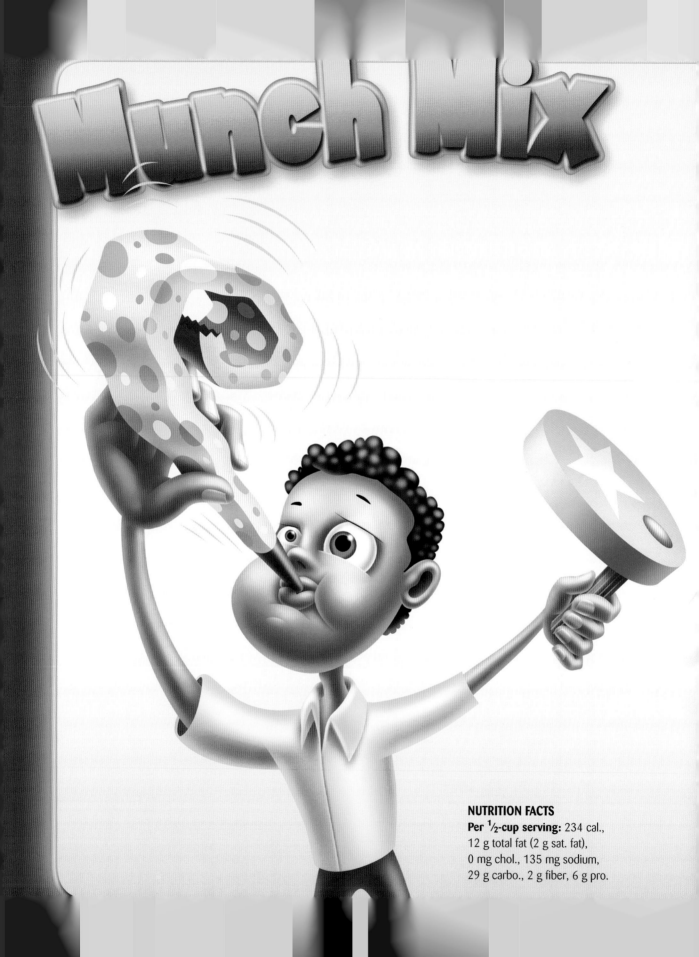

NUTRITION FACTS
Per ¹/₂-cup serving: 234 cal.,
12 g total fat (2 g sat. fat),
0 mg chol., 135 mg sodium,
29 g carbo., 2 g fiber, 6 g pro.

Utensils

Measuring cups

Large resealable plastic bag

Ingredients

1½ cups puffed corn cereal, round toasted oat cereal, or crispy corn and rice cereal

1 cup honey-roasted peanuts

½ cup candy-coated milk chocolate pieces or chewy fruit snacks

½ cup raisins

How To Make It

1 Put the cereal, peanuts, fruit snacks, and raisins in the plastic bag. Close the bag tightly. Shake well to mix.

2 Store mix in the plastic bag in a cool, dry place for up to 2 weeks. Makes 3½ cups.

You'll be right on target to satisfy everyone's hunger with this combo of crispy cereal, crunchy nuts, and chewy fruit!

Chocolate-Peanut Butter Swirls

Ingredients

1 cup graham cracker crumbs

½ cup peanuts, finely chopped

3 tablespoons butter, melted

¼ cup tub-style light cream cheese

2 tablespoons creamy peanut butter

2 tablespoons fat-free milk

2 cups fat-free milk

1 4-serving-size package sugar-free instant chocolate pudding mix

Utensils

2 small bowls

Measuring cups

Measuring spoons

Spoon

Large bowl

Wire whisk

Six 4- to 6-ounce glasses

Table knife

Plastic wrap

How To Make It

1 In a small bowl combine graham cracker crumbs and peanuts. Stir in butter until combined; save until Step 4.

2 In another small bowl stir together cream cheese and peanut butter until smooth. Gradually stir in 2 tablespoons milk until smooth. Save until Step 4.

3 In a large bowl whisk together 2 cups milk and pudding mix until combined. Continue whisking for 2 minutes.

4 Sprinkle 1 tablespoon crumb mixture into each glass. Top with a rounded tablespoon of pudding. Put a small spoonful of peanut butter mixture on top of pudding. If you like, swirl with a table knife. Top with remaining pudding and peanut butter mixture, swirling, if desired, then top with remaining crumbs.

5 Cover with plastic wrap and chill about 2 hours or until set. Makes 6 servings.

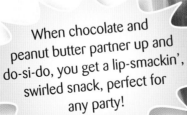

When chocolate and peanut butter partner up and do-si-do, you get a lip-smackin', swirled snack, perfect for any party!

NUTRITION FACTS
Per serving: 277 cal., 15 g total fat (7 g sat. fat), 27 mg chol., 446 mg sodium, 28 g carbo., 1 g fiber, 7 g pro.

Great Egg Bake

NUTRITION FACTS
Per serving: 224 cal., 11 g total fat (5 g sat. fat),
233 mg chol., 439 mg sodium, 16 g carbo.,
0 g fiber, 5 g pro.

Utensils

2-quart rectangular baking dish

2 table knives

4-cup measuring cup or medium bowl

Measuring cups

Measuring spoons

Rotary beater or fork

Plastic wrap

Hot pads

Wire cooling rack

Ingredients

    Shortening

6   slices bread

1   2$\frac{1}{2}$-ounce package very thinly sliced cooked ham

$\frac{1}{2}$ cup shredded cheddar cheese

6   eggs

1$\frac{1}{4}$ cups milk

$\frac{1}{8}$ teaspoon black pepper

How To Make It

1   Grease the 2-quart rectangular baking dish with shortening. Tear bread into bite-size pieces. Sprinkle half of the bread pieces into the bottom of the baking dish.

2   Cut ham into bite-size pieces using a table knife (you should have about $\frac{1}{2}$ cup). Sprinkle ham and cheese over bread in baking dish. Sprinkle remaining torn bread over ham and cheese.

3   Crack eggs into the 4-cup measuring cup or bowl. Add milk and pepper to eggs. Mix with the rotary beater or fork until whites, yolks, and other ingredients are well mixed. Pour egg mixture over bread layers in the baking dish. Cover dish with plastic wrap.

4   Chill in the refrigerator at least 2 hours but not more than 24 hours.

5   Turn on the oven to 325°F. Remove plastic wrap from baking dish. Put dish in the oven. Bake for 35 minutes.

6   Use a hot pad to pull out oven rack slightly. To see if food is cooked, stick a table knife into the center of the food in the dish. If the knife comes out clean, remove baking dish from oven using hot pads. If it does not come out clean, bake 2 to 3 minutes longer and test again. Turn off oven. Place baking dish on the cooling rack and let cool 10 minutes. Cut into squares to serve. Makes 10 servings.

There won't be any egg on your face when this dish comes out of the oven, and your parents will be stunned by your "eggcellent" cooking skills!

easy
Mac 'n' Cheese

NUTRITION FACTS
Per serving: 436 cal.,
18 g total fat (11 g sat. fat),
54 mg chol., 889 mg sodium,
45 g carbo., 3 g fiber, 21 g pro.

Utensils

Cutting board

Sharp knife

Measuring cups

Large saucepan

Hot pads

Colander

Wooden spoon

Ingredients

1   small onion

6   ounces American cheese slices

2   cups corkscrew macaroni
(rotini) or elbow macaroni

½   cup fat-free milk

½   cup frozen peas

Dash pepper

Grated Parmesan cheese,
if you like

How To Make It

1   On the cutting board use the sharp knife to cut onion into small pieces (you should have ¼ cup). Save for Step 3.

2   Tear cheese slices into bite-size pieces. Save for Step 5.

3   Cook macaroni in the saucepan following the package directions, except add onion to water along with the uncooked macaroni so they cook together. (To test macaroni for doneness, remove one piece, let it cool slightly, and bite into it. The center will be soft, not chewy.) When macaroni is cooked, turn off the burner. Remove saucepan from burner using hot pads.

4   Place colander in sink. Carefully pour macaroni mixture into the colander to drain water.

5   Return warm macaroni mixture to saucepan. Use wooden spoon to stir in cheese, milk, peas, and pepper.

6   Put saucepan on a burner. Turn the burner to medium heat. Cook for 4 to 5 minutes or until cheese is melted, stirring all the time. Turn off burner. Remove saucepan from burner. If you like, sprinkle with Parmesan cheese. Makes 3 servings.

If you're feeling cheesy, try this surefire favorite. Put a new spin on this classic by sprinkling it with peas!

Ham 'n' Cheesy Calzones

NUTRITION FACTS
Per calzone: 141 cal., 6 g total fat (3 g sat. fat), 21 mg chol., 410 mg sodium, 13 g carbo., 1 g fiber, 8 g pro.

Utensils

Baking sheet

Foil

Medium bowl

Measuring cups

Wooden spoon

Rolling pin

Sharp knife

Spoon

Fork

Measuring spoons

Pastry brush

Hot pads

Ingredients

Nonstick cooking spray

$1\frac{1}{4}$ cups chopped sliced cooked ham or turkey breast

1 cup packaged broccoli florets

$\frac{3}{4}$ cup shredded cheddar cheese (6 ounces)

1 10-ounce package refrigerated pizza dough

1 tablespoon milk

How To Make It

1 Turn on oven to 400°F. Line a baking sheet with foil; lightly coat the foil with cooking spray. Save until Step 3.

2 For filling, in medium bowl use the wooden spoon to combine ham, broccoli, and cheese.

3 On a lightly floured surface unroll pizza dough. Roll dough into a 12-inch square. Using a sharp knife, cut into nine 4-inch squares. Spoon about $\frac{1}{3}$ cup filling onto each of the squares. Moisten edges of dough with water. Fold dough over filling from corner to corner. Press edges of dough with tines of a fork to seal. Use the fork to prick holes in the top of each calzone to allow steam to escape. Place calzones on baking sheet. Brush with milk using pastry brush.

4 Put baking sheet in oven. Bake for 13 to 15 minutes or until golden. Turn off oven. Use hot pads to remove baking sheet from oven. Serve warm. Makes 9 calzones.

Go ahead, ham it up! Loaded with ham, broccoli, and cheese, these pockets pack a punch!

Super Sub

Utensils

Cutting board

Serrated knife

Measuring spoons

Table knife

Measuring cups

Ingredients

1   hoagie bun

2   tablespoons light sour cream ranch dip or your favorite bottled ranch salad dressing

¼   cup shredded carrot

¼   cup shredded lettuce

¼   cup shredded, seeded cucumber

2   ounces thinly sliced assorted deli meats (such as roast beef, ham, or turkey)

1   ounce thinly sliced mozzarella, American, or provolone cheese

How To Make It

1   Split hoagie bun lengthwise, if necessary, using the serrated knife. Use the table knife to spread cut sides of bread with dip or salad dressing. Layer carrot, lettuce, cucumber, meat, and cheese on bottom portion of bread. Top with the other portion of bread. Makes 1 serving.

NUTRITION FACTS
Per serving: 652 cal., 23 g total fat (9 g sat. fat), 76 mg chol., 941 mg sodium, 79 g carbo., 5 g fiber, 34 g pro.

Take the plunge and use this piled-high sub to sink your hunger!

Rockin' Tuna Sandwiches

NUTRITION FACTS
Per serving (2 sandwiches): 228 cal., 7 g total fat (1 g sat. fat),
24 mg chol., 599 mg sodium, 27 g carbo., 3 g fiber, 16 g pro.

Utensils

Can opener

Small bowl

Spoon

Measuring cups

Measuring spoons

Cutting board

4- to $4\frac{1}{2}$-inch cookie cutter

Table knife

Ingredients

1   3-ounce can chunk white tuna in water, drained and flaked

½   cup packaged shredded cabbage with carrot (coleslaw mix)

2   tablespoons plain low-fat yogurt

2   tablespoons bottled reduced-fat ranch salad dressing

8   thin slices whole grain bread

     Capers, sliced pimiento-stuffed olives, and/or raisins, if you like

How To Make It

1   In the small bowl use a spoon to combine tuna and cabbage mix. Stir in yogurt and salad dressing.

2   Using the cookie cutter, cut fish or other shapes from bread slices. Save bread scraps for another use. Spread tuna mixture on half of the bread shapes using the table knife. Top with remaining bread shapes. If you like, decorate sandwiches with capers, olives, and/ or raisins. Can chill up to 24 hours. Makes 2 servings.

These sandwiches are a swimming good time. Make them in all kinds of shapes, including fish shapes!

83

Totally Trick Tacos

Utensils

Large skillet with lid

Wooden spoon

Colander

2 medium bowls

Disposable container
for fat

Measuring cups

Measuring spoons

Spoon

Baking sheet,
if heating taco shells

Hot pads,
if heating taco shells

Tongs,
if heating taco shells

NUTRITION FACTS
Per serving (2 tacos) : 329 cal.,
19 g total fat (9 g sat. fat),
75 mg chol., 350 mg sodium,
15 g carbo., 1 g fiber, 22 g pro.

Ingredients

12 ounces lean ground beef

½ cup salsa

½ teaspoon dried oregano, crushed

4 lettuce leaves

8 regular-size taco shells*

¾ cup shredded cheddar cheese (3 ounces)

Dairy sour cream, chopped tomato, and salsa, if you like

How To Make It

1 Put ground beef in the skillet; use the wooden spoon to break up meat. Put the skillet on a burner. Turn the burner to medium-high heat. Cook until no pink color is left in meat, stirring now and then with the wooden spoon. This will take 8 to 10 minutes. Turn off burner. Remove skillet from burner.

2 Place colander over a bowl. Spoon meat into the colander and let the fat drain into the bowl. Spoon meat back into skillet. Put fat in a container to throw away.

3 Stir ½ cup salsa and the oregano into meat. Cover skillet and put skillet on a burner. Turn the burner to medium heat. Cook for 5 minutes, stirring with the wooden spoon after about 3 minutes. Turn off burner. Remove skillet from burner. Put meat in a bowl.

4 While meat mixture is cooking, tear or cut lettuce into bite-size pieces.

5 To make tacos, spoon some of the meat mixture into a taco shell. Add lettuce and cheese. If you like, top with sour cream, chopped tomato, and extra salsa.

*If you like, make taco shells crisp by placing them on a baking sheet and warming them in a 350°F oven for 5 to 7 minutes or until they are the desired crispness. Turn off oven. Use hot pads to remove baking sheet from oven. Use tongs to put shells on a cool plate. Makes 4 servings.

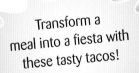

Transform a meal into a fiesta with these tasty tacos!

Utensils

Foil

Can opener

Colander, if you use black beans

Medium bowl, if you use black beans

Potato masher, if you use black beans

Medium saucepan

Wooden spoon

Hot pads

Measuring cups

Measuring spoons

Ingredients

4   10-inch flour tortillas

1   16-ounce can refried beans or
     one 15-ounce can black beans

$\frac{1}{4}$ teaspoon cumin

$\frac{1}{2}$ cup salsa or picante sauce

$\frac{1}{2}$ cup shredded taco cheese
     or cheddar cheese (2 ounces)

$\frac{1}{2}$ cup lettuce torn in small pieces

     Additional salsa or picante sauce,
     if you like

NUTRITION FACTS
Per serving: 323 cal., 10 g total fat
(4 g sat. fat), 15 mg chol.,
860 mg sodium, 36 g carbo.,
6 g fiber, 14 g pro.

How To Make It

1   Turn on the oven to 350°F. Wrap tortillas in foil. Put wrapped tortillas in oven. Bake about 10 minutes or until tortillas are warm.

2   Open can of beans. (If you are using black beans, pour beans into a colander, rinse with cold water, and drain thoroughly. Put black beans into the bowl and mash them with the potato masher.) Put refried beans or mashed black beans into the saucepan. Stir cumin into beans. Put the saucepan on the burner. Turn the burner to medium heat. Cook about 5 minutes or until beans are warm, stirring now and then with the wooden spoon. Turn off burner. Remove saucepan from burner.

3   Turn off oven. Use hot pads to remove tortillas from oven.

4   Spoon about $\frac{1}{4}$ cup of the beans near one edge of each tortilla. Add 2 tablespoons salsa, 2 tablespoons cheese, and 2 tablespoons lettuce. Roll tortillas around filling. If you like, serve with additional salsa or picante sauce. Makes 4 servings.

If your stomach is feeling empty, stuff it with a loaded burrito and you'll be saying, "cool beans!"

Star Pizza

NUTRITION FACTS
Per serving: 254 cal., 9 g total fat (3 g sat. fat),
28 mg chol., 851 mg sodium, 27 g carbo.,
1 g fiber, 18 g pro.

Utensils

Pizza pan or baking sheet

Measuring spoons

Spoon

Cutting board

Sharp knife or kitchen scissors

Star-shape cookie cutter

Hot pads

Wire cooling rack

Pancake turner

Ingredients

1 4-ounce Italian bread shell (such as Boboli)

2 tablespoons pizza sauce

2 slices Canadian-style bacon or large pepperoni (1 to 2 ounces)

3 thin slices mozzarella cheese and/or cheddar cheese ($1\frac{1}{2}$ ounces)

How To Make It

1 Turn on the oven to 425°F. Put the Italian bread shell on the pizza pan or baking sheet.

2 Drizzle the pizza sauce over the bread shell. Use the back of the spoon to spread the pizza sauce over the bread shell to within $\frac{1}{2}$ inch of the edge.

3 Put the Canadian-style bacon or pepperoni slices on the cutting board. Cut the bacon or pepperoni into $\frac{3}{4}$-inch-wide strips with the sharp knife or scissors. Arrange the meat strips on the pizza to make 3 stripes.

4 Put the cheese slices on the cutting board. Use the star-shape cutter to cut the cheese. Place the cheese stars on the pizza.

5 Put the pan in the oven. Bake for 5 to 7 minutes or until pizza is hot. Turn off the oven. Use the hot pads to remove the pizza pan from the oven. Place the pan on the cooling rack.

6 Cut the pizza into wedges with the sharp knife. Use the pancake turner to transfer the pizza to the serving plates. Serve immediately. Makes 2 servings.

Meat, cheese, sauce, and crust play the starring roles, but you're sure to take top billing with this pizza pie!

Outrageously Sloppy Joes

Utensils

Large skillet

Wooden spoon

Colander

Medium bowl

Disposable
  container for fat

Can opener

Small rubber spatula

Small storage
  container with lid

Measuring cups

Cutting board

Sharp knife

Measuring spoons

Spoon

NUTRITION FACTS
Per serving:
255 cal., 8 g total fat (3 g sat. fat),
39 mg chol., 414 mg sodium,
29 g carbo., 3 g fiber, 16 g pro.

Ingredients

12 ounces lean ground beef

½ of a 15-ounce can refried beans

1 4½-ounce can diced green chile peppers, drained, if you like

½ cup bottled salsa

1 small onion

¼ cup water

½ teaspoon bottled minced garlic

6 hamburger buns, split

Shredded cheddar cheese, shredded lettuce, sliced pitted ripe olives, sliced pickles, and/or dairy sour cream, if you like

These saucy sandwiches may get a little sloppy, but their kicked-up flavor will knock your socks off!

How To Make It

1   Put ground beef in the skillet. Break up meat with the wooden spoon. Put the skillet on a burner. Turn the burner to medium-high heat. Cook until no pink color is left in the meat, stirring now and then with the wooden spoon. This will take 8 to 10 minutes. Turn off burner. Remove skillet from burner.

2   Place colander over the bowl. Spoon meat into the colander and let the fat drain into the bowl. Spoon meat back into skillet. Put fat in a container to throw away.

3   Use the can opener to open the refried beans and, if you like, the green chile peppers. Use a rubber spatula to scrape half of the refried beans (about ¾ cup) and all the chile peppers into the skillet. Put remaining beans in a tightly covered container and refrigerate for another use. Add the salsa to the skillet. On the cutting board use the sharp knife to cut the onion into small pieces (you should have ⅓ cup). Add onion, water, and minced garlic to the skillet.

4   Put the skillet on a burner. Turn the burner to medium-high heat. Cook until the mixture comes to boiling, stirring now and then with wooden spoon. Turn the burner to low heat. Cook about 10 to 15 minutes or until the mixture is thick and most of the liquid is gone, stirring now and then. Turn off burner.

5   Spoon the meat mixture into buns. If you like, top with cheese, lettuce, olives, pickles, and/or sour cream. Serve immediately. Makes 6 servings.

Crispy Chicken Dippers

Utensils

3 small bowls

Measuring cups

Measuring spoons

Spoon

Plastic wrap

2 1-quart resealable
  plastic bags

Rolling pin

Cutting board

Sharp knife

Large baking sheet

Hot pads

Waxed paper, if warming
  honey-mustard sauce

NUTRITION FACTS
Per serving: 354 cal., 10 g total fat (2 g sat. fat),
126 mg chol., 637 mg sodium, 34 g carbo., 2 g fiber, 31 g pro.

Ingredients

½ cup low-fat mayonnaise dressing or salad dressing

4 teaspoons Dijon-style mustard

1 tablespoon honey

30 whole wheat or regular rich, round crackers, finely crushed (1¼ cups)

1 pound skinless, boneless chicken breast halves

¼ cup all-purpose flour

1 teaspoon dried parsley flakes

½ teaspoon poultry seasoning

⅛ teaspoon salt

   Dash black pepper

1 egg, beaten

2 tablespoons milk

How To Make It

1 Turn on oven to 425°F.

2 For honey-mustard sauce, in a bowl stir together mayonnaise, mustard, and honey. Cover with plastic wrap and chill until serving time.

3 Put crackers in a resealable plastic bag. Seal bag. Use the rolling pin to crush the crackers into fine crumbs. Pour crackers into small bowl. Save crackers until Step 5.

4 On the cutting board use the sharp knife to cut chicken into 1½-inch pieces. In another plastic bag combine flour, parsley flakes, poultry seasoning, salt, and pepper. Add chicken pieces, a few at a time, to the flour mixture. Close the bag; shake to coat chicken pieces. Save chicken until Step 5.

5 In a bowl stir together egg and milk. Dip coated chicken pieces, a few at a time, into the egg mixture. Roll the pieces in crackers. Place in a single layer on an ungreased baking sheet. Place in oven and bake for 10 to 12 minutes or until chicken is no longer pink. Turn off oven. Use hot pads to remove baking sheet from the oven.

6 Serve with cold or warm honey-mustard sauce. To warm sauce, cover with waxed paper and microwave on 100% power (high) for 30 seconds or until heated through. (Or transfer sauce to a small saucepan and stir over low heat.)
Makes 4 servings.

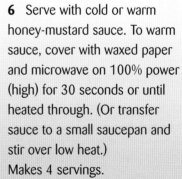

Don't get burned by long wait times at restaurants. Make your own crispy dippers and eat them whenever you want!

 Index

THIS BOOK BELONGS TO

_____